MW01002748

ARE THERE TERRORISTS iN YOUR CHURCH?

by Tom Kraeuter

TRAINING RESOURCES
8929 Old LeMay Ferry Rd.
Hillsboro, MO 63050

P.O. Box 635, Lynnwood WA 98046

Are There Terrorists in Your Church?
by Tom Kraeuter

© 2005 Training Resources, Inc.
8929 Old LeMay Ferry Road
Hillsboro, MO 63050
(636) 789-4522
www.training-resources.org

ISBN # 1-932096-31-0

Printed in the United States of America.

Other Books by Tom Kraeuter

If Standing Together Is So Great,
Why Do We Keep Falling Apart?

Living Beyond the Ordinary:
Developing an Extraordinary Relationship with God

Worship Is...What?!

Oh, Grow Up!
The Everyday Miracle of Becoming More Like Jesus

Times of Refreshing – A Worship Ministry Devotional

Keys to Becoming an Effective Worship Leader

Guiding Your Church Through a Worship Transition

Developing an Effective Worship Ministry

The Worship Leader's Handbook

Things They Didn't Teach Me in Worship Leading School

To order any of these books or for information about the
teaching ministry of Tom Kraeuter, please contact:

> Training Resources, Inc.
> 8929 Old LeMay Ferry Road
> Hillsboro, MO 63050
> 636-789-4522
> www.training-resources.org
> staff@training-resources.org

Dedication

I humbly dedicate this book to my son, Stephen.

Stephen, my interaction with you has taught me much about relating with others. Believe it or not, I've learned a lot from you (and most has been good!). Your quick wit and constant humor are a joy. Your 110% attitude has been an inspiration to me and to others. I thank God that He placed you in our family.

I am proud to call you my son!

Acknowledgments

Thanks to the scores of people who reviewed the manuscript ahead of time and offered valuable feedback. Among these, some of the most notable input was offered by Les Young, Bill Stiebs and George Heil.

Thanks to the numerous pastors and leaders who have endured terrorist attacks, whose stories gave me the impetus to write this book.

Thanks to Jamie Allebach and Allebach Creative Associates, Souderton, Pennsylvania, for the great cover design and artwork.

Thanks to Lois Schachner for excellent proofing and final edit suggestions.

Special thanks to Jennifer Brody for another great editing job.

And, of course, thanks to my family, Barbara, David, Stephen and Amy, for loving me all the way through the time-consuming writing of another book.

Contents

Introduction

On December 7, 1941, our nation was violently and maliciously attacked by another country. Nearly sixty years later—September 11, 2001—our nation was attacked again. This time, however, it was not by another country. The attack was from a group of independent terrorists. Interestingly, at least for those of us with a more religious perspective, the aggressors were not just trying to be destructive for the sake of destruction. They honestly believed that by attacking, they were doing the will of God.

Have you ever encountered terrorists in your church? No, I'm not talking about guys walking around with AK47s, ready to blast people to smithereens. Church terrorists don't highjack jets or use explosives. They don't wear camouflage clothing or look through night vision goggles for clandestine attacks. These church terrorists, however, are just as destructive.

Would you like to know what's really alarming about most church terrorists? They don't even realize that they are involved in terrorism. Most of the time they glibly go about destroying churches while thinking they are doing the right thing. They have no clue as to the horrendously destructive consequences of their actions. The truth is, though, that their words are actually more injurious than any gun or hand grenade. The seeds they plant in the minds of their hearers will ultimately prove to be every bit as fatal as a 747 loaded with jet fuel.

Who are these terrorists? Well, I don't want to alarm you, but they may be all around you. In fact, you could be one of them. No, this is not a new version of a B-grade alien body snatchers movie. This is serious business. Very serious business. The Body of Christ is under attack. Sadly, the foremost attack is coming from within.

I have encountered terrorists in Bible-believing churches of nearly every background all across North America. They might be Baptist or Mennonite. They could be Pentecostal, Nazarene, Methodist, Vineyard or Lutheran. Now don't get smug if the name of your group isn't listed. I just don't have time or space to list them all. They all, however, have experienced attacks from terrorists.

Nearly every pastor to whom I have posed the question, "Are there terrorists in your church?" has responded, "Yes." Interestingly, not all church terrorists are obvious or blatant. Most you would never, ever suspect. One pastor told about the mild-mannered, elderly widow who sits in the back pew. She didn't like the way *her* church was changing and set out to stop the changes at any cost. Another shared about a recent college graduate who, with such a great education under his belt, now knew pretty much all there was to know. Consequently he decided to "fix" the church in which he grew up. It wasn't a pretty situation. Of course there are lots of other stories, far too many to mention. Some are so bizarre that they are almost unbelievable.

In fact, there was a time when I nearly became a church terrorist. I was convinced the leadership of our church wasn't handling a particular situation well. So, in a not-too-delicate manner, I confronted. Heated words were spoken. Pushy emails were sent. Long-time relationships were on the verge of crumbling. It had the potential of becoming an ugly scenario. Fortunately, the Lord's mercy intervened. In retrospect, I am aghast at how close I came to severely damaging the work of God.

The tragic lesson is that we all have the ability—and, in our sinful nature, the inclination—to be church terrorists. Sometimes it is intentional. Other times we can unwittingly become involved in terrorist activities in the church. Regardless, those activities can be horrendously destructive.

This book is an attempt to expose the attack, and, more importantly, to show how to stop it. If you have ever wanted to see the Church truly fulfill the plans and purposes of God, this book will offer a giant step toward making that reality.

By the way, the first three chapters are a fictional story that lay a foundation for the remainder of the book. After that I'll make application about what you read in the story. I hope you enjoy it, but more importantly, I pray that you find practical answers for your life and your church.

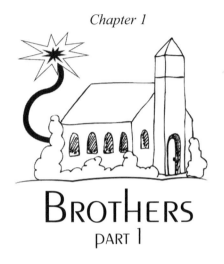

Chapter 1

BROTHERS
PART 1

"Pass the rice, will you Julie?" Bill Spencer looked tired. He had a lot on his mind these days. Not only was the company he worked for facing more than its share of economic woes, but he was also encountering significant problems at church as well. "I still can't stop thinking about what Jim Crandall said about Pastor Wallace." Bill paused and looked directly at his wife. "You know, I really think he's right. I mean, how can the guy pastor a church for eight years and not have something of significance to show for it? Our attendance is about the same as it was when he came, and I really can't honestly say I've seen much change in people's lives. There must be some reason God isn't blessing his ministry."

Bill and Julie Spencer had been a part of Johnsonville Community Church for more than a dozen years. They found the church after moving to the area because of a job change. Both of them had jumped right into ministry opportunities, teaching Sunday School and singing in the choir. Bill had even been a part of the search committee that had recommended Pastor Wallace. Now, nearly a decade later, he was sure the committee had made a mistake.

"He's, like, nowhere near as good a preacher as the guy over at First Church," said teenage Kyle. "Their church is growing like crazy."

"That's true, son," responded Dad. "But Pastor Wallace's preaching ability is only part of the picture. There's more than just that."

"I agree, dear. Ramona Heinz said the same thing this afternoon at our Bible study. She thinks he might be..." Julie glanced at their children, then back at Bill. "...that he might be...doing things he shouldn't be doing."

"Why does she think that?" inquired Bill.

"Well, Ramona said she had thought there was something not quite right. Then last week she was driving past the Rodriguez's house and saw Pastor Wallace leaving the house alone late at night."

"So?" Bill looked a bit confused.

"Well, don't you remember? Armando has been working in Central America for the past month. He's not home. And pastor is at their house late at night? What would you think?"

"Yeah, Mom, but that's just, you know, circumspectual evidence." When they first came to Johnsonville, Kyle was just three years old. Now he was a know-it-all teenager.

"The word is circum*stantial*, Kyle," replied his father. "And although it is only circumstantial evidence, when you put all the pieces together it sounds like a pretty strong case."

"May I please be excused?" The request was from seven-year-old Shelly. She was generally quiet and somewhat shy compared with big brother Kyle and their mom and dad.

"Not yet, honey," said Dad. "We haven't read our Scripture verse, and we're going to start reading a new story tonight. This book," Bill pulled a story book out of a bag next to his chair, "has become very popular. It's a new book by one of my favorite authors, Tex Arcado. I thought we should read it together as a family. It's called *Brothers*."

"That sounds like fun," said Mom. "Okay, whose turn is it to pick the Bible verse?"

"It was my turn last night," said Dad. "That means it must be Kyle's turn." He handed the small, bread-shaped holder to Kyle. The young man eyed the little multi-colored cards sticking out and snatched one out of the middle.

Kyle looked at the card and then began reading in a monotone voice. "James 4:11. 'Brothers, do not slander one another. Anyone who speaks against his brother or judges him speaks against the law and judges it. When you judge the

law, you are not keeping it, but sitting in judgment on it.'"
Kyle paused looking rather bewildered, then added, "Did
that, like, make any sense at all?"

His mother looked at him and smiled. "Well, Kyle, the
first part is pretty simple. Here, let me see the card." Kyle
gladly handed the card to his mother, and she read it. "Yes,
'Brothers, do not slander one another.' That means not to say
bad things about other people."

"Yeah, I got that part. It's what's after it, that stuff about,
you know, speaking judgment on the law, or whatever. I just
don't get it."

"Well, Kyle," began Mom, "it says, 'Anyone who
speaks against his brother or judges him speaks against the
law and judges it. When you judge the law, you are not keeping it, but sitting in judgment on it.' What that means is that
if you say bad things about a brother in Christ, it's the same
as sitting in judgment on the commands of God. That's how
bad it is to say nasty things about fellow Christians."

"That's right. We all need to be very careful about how
we talk about one another," added Dad.

Shelly's wide-eyed innocence got the best of her. She
didn't mean to cause awkward moments so frequently. It was
just that she wanted to understand things but often didn't. Her
seven-year-old mind couldn't seem to keep up with the rest
of the family. "So does that mean the stuff you said about
Pastor Wallace before?"

Mom glanced at Dad, searching for a response. There
was a moment of silence and then Dad answered, "That's a

little different, honey. We'll explain it to you some other time." Dad reached down and grabbed the book next to his chair. "Right now," he said, "let's read part of this new story." With that he opened the book and began to read.

The air was hot and heavy as Jamar stood staring up at the mountain. Actually it wasn't just *a* mountain at all. It was one very large mountain surrounded by four other smaller ones. It was the dream fortress of every military commander. A handful of men strategically placed could ward off an entire battalion indefinitely. If Jamar could have designed it himself he would have changed almost nothing. But he was not one of those *on* the mountain. He stood in the valley below staring up at it. On the mountain was the kingdom of Lachish.

Our final conquest, thought Jamar. *The only place we have yet to conquer*. His thoughts were interrupted by yet another messenger bringing a request to the Commander-in-Chief.

The message was delivered succinctly but breathlessly. "The king...of Ustanol would...like... to meet with...you, Sire." The messenger was a young man, not much more than a boy. The sweat poured off of him as he gasped for breath. His small frame and fair complexion did not suit his task. He was sunburned and exhausted. Ustanol was more than three days walk to the west—

through the desert. Making the journey quickly was no easy job.

"*King* of Ustanol?!" Jamar acted surprised. "How can a conquered people have a *king*?" he asked, more to himself than to the lad. Jamar stared off in the direction of Ustanol. "What does he want?"

The boy stammered at first, but finally said, "He...would...like to discuss...a few...of the terms... of the treaty." At the final phrase the young man cowered a bit, as though expecting to be struck.

Jamar looked at the youth. "Oh, he wants to discuss the terms of the treaty, does he?" His voice sounded facetious. "And what exactly does he expect to gain from such a meeting? I personally told him how to write the treaty, and he signed it. It seems to me that there really isn't any room for negotiation." Jamar turned and stared off into the distance again, deep in thought. Although he sometimes displayed a gruff exterior, Jamar was actually a benevolent ruler. Finally, he looked at the winded youth and smiled. "Yes," said Jamar, "Tell your *king* I will grant him safe passage to come and meet with me next week."

The young man paused for just a second to make sure he hadn't misheard Jamar. Then, suddenly, he looked as though he had just had his death sentence commuted. "Thank you, sir." He bowed low. Over and over the lad repeated, "Thank you, sir. Thank you." He kept bowing and thanking until he was completely out of Jamar's sight. Jamar found the entire scenario so humorous that he laughed until his sides hurt. Later, he related the story to one of his officers, and laughed again. The thought of the sunburned, worn-out boy bowing and thanking him repeatedly was perhaps the funniest thing Jamar had seen in quite some time.

"I wish I would have been there," choked out Shomo between laughs. Shomo was Jamar's best friend. Like Jamar, Shomo was intelligent, quick-witted and thoroughly enjoyed a good laugh.

"I'm sure you would have broken out in laughter right then and there, Shomo. The boy could not stop thanking me. I truly think he expected to die." Jamar paused and looked out the window. The laughter left his face. "But now it is time to talk of more serious matters. We must make plans to take the mountain...and the treasure."

A large man with coal-black hair and deep-set, dark eyes, Jamar Leōn was as strong as an ox and more than handsome. He was known as Jamar the Spirited Conqueror. He had never lost a battle but could be as giddy and fun-loving as a child. His reputation was recognized far and wide. In the few short years of his reign he had brought the entire region—north to Dunirk, as far south as the Soldon

River, east past the Sudilin Mountains and as far west as Ustanol—under his domain. He was a brilliant strategist and a natural leader. People followed Jamar because, well, because he was Jamar. There was something about him that made folks want to follow. He had led his armies and conquered almost every kingdom in the region. Some had simply given up when they saw him coming. The people of Asherese ran out to greet him and willingly became his subjects. Others, like Ustanol, had put up resistance, but it was always futile. Jamar would win. Jamar would always win.

Interestingly, though, he disliked shedding blood if it could be avoided. He really did not relish the idea of killing people. Jamar genuinely cared for his subjects and would always endeavor to find a way to avoid conflict if possible. He cared for the people, and the people loved him for it.

Jamar had grown up here in Zarasitong. Plants and wildlife were plentiful in the beautiful valley. The people had everything they could ever need. Crops grew in abundance. Hunting was bountiful. All of these combined with the almost unbelievably mild weather reminded one of living in paradise.

When Jamar saw how others lived outside of Zarasitong, he felt sorry for them. Dunirk was nearly always terribly wet. Ustanol and Feronere were on the edge of the desert. Almost nothing grew in the Sudilin mountains. The more Jamar traveled, the more he realized just how much Zarasitong really was a paradise.

In fact, that was one of Jamar's main motivations in conquering. He wanted others to have the same benefits he had. If he could open up trade routes and people could travel unhindered, it would add good things to their lives, he reasoned.

That was only part of the reason for Jamar's conquests, though. Yes, Jamar had grown up in the beautiful Zarasitong valley, but he had also grown up in the shadow of Lachish mountain. Indeed, the only place more alluring to the people of Zarasitong—and Jamar—was Lachish. Lachish had everything the valley had with the added benefit of the natural protection. And the treasure.

No one knew exactly what the treasure was, but *everyone* knew it was there. Beneath a huge boulder on the very top of the mountain lay wealth untold. Nearly all who had ever heard about the treasure had considered how they could get it, but they all realized the futility of it. Attacking a place like Lachish would be suicide. Everyone knew it.

Jamar stared out the window at the mountain as he had done thousands of times throughout his lifetime. His eyes squinted as the evening sun hung over Lachish. He had always wanted to go up there but his parents told him—everyone in Zarasitong knew—that it wasn't safe. No one seemed to have much firsthand knowledge about the people of Lachish. But there were *lots* of stories and rumors.

Jamar's thoughts drifted back to a time when he was just a boy. Jamar was the youngest of eight children. The rest were all girls. His father, the king of Zarasitong, desperately wanted a son to succeed him on the throne. But one girl followed another until Jamrael had nearly given up. Finally, his wife had presented him with a baby boy. Jamar.

Jamar had grown and was probably six or seven years old when his oldest sister was nearly a woman. "A very beautiful young lady," all the people said. Outgoing and friendly, Sherene became the talk of the valley. She was every young man's dream. Lovely, vivacious, enchanting, Sherene embodied all of these and more. But then, all of a sudden she was missing for several days. Jamar wondered why, but no one told him anything. The adults and older children talked in hushed tones, but Jamar, as the baby, knew nothing. Only much later did he find out that Sherene had left home to marry a man from Lachish.

Jamrael Leon had consented to the marriage with the hope of fostering better relationships between the two kingdoms. Sherene married one of the sons of the king of Lachish, but the union never seemed to have the desired effect. In fact, since Sherene was so popular among the people of the valley, her leaving to live on the mountain actually seemed to create more animosity toward the mountain people.

"So how and when do you propose we attack?"

"Huh?" Jamar looked bewilderedly toward Shomo.

"The mountain. How and when will we take it?"

"Oh, sorry," said Jamar sheepishly. "I guess my mind wandered off for a minute."

"Wandered off? Actually, I thought you were sleeping with your eyes open. Where exactly was it that you 'wandered off' to, Jamar?"

"I was up on the mountain, Shomo. But I was much younger than I am now."

"Sherene?" Shomo knew Jamar well. They had few secrets from one another. Friends since childhood, Shomo and Jamar could see right through one another.

"Yes," admitted Jamar. "I wish she never would have gone." He paused. "Why did my father agree to the wedding? At least it could have been held publicly. The secrecy made the whole thing far worse." Jamar looked directly at his friend. "Shomo, isn't it ironic? Here we are facing what may well be the biggest battle of our lives, and the whole thing might have been completely avoided if just a couple of details in history were different." Shomo nodded.

The two men sat quietly considering things that might have been.

*   *   *   *   *   *

Ramiel stood on the balcony looking out over the valley. "Sherene, why don't we try again to reach out to your people. Surely they cannot still hold a grudge, can they?"

"I don't know, Ramiel." Sherene, still as lovely as ever after nearly thirty years of marriage, sighed, "I certainly hope not."

"We have so much to offer them. And they, too, have much we can learn. It seems so ridiculous that we can be this close and yet be so completely separated. I wish there was something we could do."

Ramiel thought back to the attempts they had made to bring about a better relationship between Lachish and Zarasitong. Their first foray into the valley together was a disaster. They were met with strong opposition. Indeed, both were fortunate to escape alive. "Kill Ramiel the thief!" the people cried. "And don't let the traitor Sherene escape either." What a rapid turn of events! The once beloved Sherene was now running like an outlaw. The young couple quickly retreated to the mountain. They were shocked at the hostility of the valley people.

Dad closed the book and said, "That's a good place to stop for tonight."

"Aw, just a little more, Daddy...please?" cooed Shelly, looking lovingly at her father.

"Not tonight, honey. I've got a meeting at church in just a little while. I need to get ready. We'll read more tomorrow." With that, the kitchen became a flurry of activity. The table was cleared, the dishwasher filled and the excess food stored in the refrigerator. Dad readied himself for his meeting, and the others went about their evening activities. But Shelly kept wondering about the Bible verse and the earlier conversation.

Chapter 2

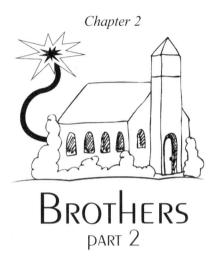

BROTHERS
PART 2

This ham is wonderful," said Bill Spencer to his wife. "Did you do something different than usual?"

"No, it was a more expensive kind than I usually buy, but it was on sale. It is really good, isn't it?"

Through a mouthful of dinner roll Kyle interjected, "Hey, do you guys know who Jane Reisner is?"

"Kyle, don't talk with your mouth full," scolded his mother. "Hmmm. Jane? Do you mean Shawn and Joni's daughter?"

Kyle swallowed and then looked blankly at his mother,

"How should I know her parents' names?" He shook his head. "She lives over on Kilding Street, just behind WalMart."

"Yes, Kyle, that's Shawn and Joni Reisner. Jane is their daughter. What about her?"

"She's got cancer."

"What?!" Julie's surprise was obvious.

"I'll say it slower, Mom." Kyle rolled his eyes. "She's... got...cancer."

"Don't be a smart aleck, Kyle," said his dad. "I think your mom was kind of shocked. We've known the Reisners for a long time."

"Do you know anything more than that, dear?" asked his mother.

"Not really. I guess she just found out."

"Well, hopefully she'll get some support from the youth group," added Mom.

"I doubt it. When she's there she, like, hangs out with the other losers," Kyle screwed up his face indicating his dislike of the "losers." "They really aren't much into what the rest of us are doing."

"Well, this might just be a good time to reach out to her. She's going to need some real friends at a time like this."

"Mom, you don't get it," Kyle frowned. "Jane is a Christian, but...just barely. She's always making bad choices and hanging with the wrong crowd." Kyle took a quick drink of milk. "She probably deserves to get cancer. God's probably punishing her or whatever."

"Now Kyle, you shouldn't say such things," responded

his mother.

"But Mom, why not? It's true."

"Uh, how about if we read our Bible verse for today," said Dad, trying to diffuse the tension. "Whose turn is it?"

"It must be Shelly's turn tonight," replied Mom.

"Okay, Shelly," Dad handed her the container of Bible cards, "pick a good one." Shelly studied the bundle of multicolored cards like a detective looking for clues.

"Dad," whined Kyle, "she always does this. Tell her to just, like, take one so we can get done."

"I'm picking one, I'm picking one," said Shelly. She studied the cards for a few more seconds and then pulled out a blue one. Shelly looked at it for a moment making sure she knew all the words and then read, "Proverbs 12:18. Reckless words pierce like a sword, but the tongue of the wise brings healing."

Dad quickly jumped up from the table and assumed a fencing stance. Then he jabbed toward Shelly with his imaginary sword. "Take that! And that!" Kyle just looked at his mom and rolled his eyes.

"Uh, Dad, what are you doing?" asked Shelly.

"I'm piercing you with a sword. Oh, okay, it's only pretend, but what if it was real? Would you like to be stabbed with a sword?"

"No."

"Of course not. It would hurt. It would probably hurt a lot. It might cause some pretty serious injuries, wouldn't it?"

"I guess so," responded Shelly, hoping it was the right answer.

"That's what this verse says about our words. If we say mean things it's like we're," Dad motioned again with his imaginary sword, "stabbing someone with a sword."

"But it goes on to say," interjected Mom, "that the tongue of the wise brings healing. Shelly, would you rather have someone do something that hurts you or something that helps heal you?"

"Well, I guess something that helps heal me."

"Right," agreed Dad. "And that's what we can do with our words. We can either hurt someone or help heal someone, depending on what we say and how we say it."

"So if we say nice things we help heal, and if we say mean things we hurt?" asked Shelly.

Dad smiled, "Exactly." *Maybe some of this stuff does get through*, he thought.

"So when Kyle said mean things about Jane was that like stabbing her with a sword?"

Kyle suddenly found himself paying attention. "That's different," blurted out Kyle. Then raising his voice, he added, "What I said was true."

"Easy Kyle. She's just asking a question."

Shelly looked confused. Once again she found herself in the position of not understanding. "So if we say mean things that are true, it's okay?"

"Well, not exactly..." began Dad.

Kyle interrupted, "How about if we read the story? I want to know what Jamar is going to do."

"Uh, maybe that's a good idea," responded Mom. Dad

picked up the book, turned to the marked page and began to read.

Ramiel heard a knock at the door of the inner chamber. "Enter," he said.

The door opened quickly and two men clamored in. One was a tall man, very thin with short, unkempt hair and wrinkled clothes. The other seemed to be his exact opposite: short, fat, bald and immaculately dressed.

"Your Highness," said the tall man excitedly, "we have found something that we think you will find interesting." He waved a large, leather-bound book toward Ramiel.

"So what is this exciting thing you have found, Moolan?" Ramiel looked at Sherene and winked. Moolan was easily excited and found the simplest things in life to be great treasures.

"It is a diary, Your Highness. It was actually found a week ago, but we wanted to try to be sure it was authentic before we brought it to you."

"Whose diary, Moolan?"

"Well, Sire, if the information is correct, and we believe it is, although we are not yet 100% sure so we do have someone else doing a bit more research, but if it proves to be accurate..."

"Moolan, will you get to the point?"

"Oh, yes. I'm sorry, Your Highness. Well, if

we're right, then this," he held the book high, "is the diary of your great-great-great-great-great-(that's five greats, Your Highness)-grandfather. His name was Lachish."

"That's very nice. I'll look forward to reading it at some point when I can spare the time."

"Excuse me, King Ramiel." The short man spoke. "With all due respect, Sire, I don't think you understand the significance of this. We believe the information in the diary is earth-shattering...in a manner of speaking."

Ramiel eyed the pair suspiciously. "What do you mean?" he asked.

It was Moolan who responded, "Well, sir if the information is correct, and we believe it is..."

"Yes, yes, Moolan. Please get to the point."

"Well, if this book is right, then Lachish is Queen Sherene's great-great-great-great-great-*uncle*. His brother was named Zarasitong."

"What?!" exclaimed Ramiel. He looked from Moolan to Sherene and back to Moolan again.

"It's true, Sire. They were brothers and came to this land to seek a new life. Once here they decided to separate. Lachish chose the mountain, Zarasitong the valley."

"This is incredible," said Ramiel.

"That's what we thought, Sire. That's why we wanted to try to be sure the information was accurate, but we aren't yet completely..."

"Yes, I know, Moolan." Ramiel sounded a bit annoyed. "You are not totally sure that it is accurate, but you believe it is." He pondered for a moment, then exclaimed, "Of course it is true! Now the treasure makes sense." He looked at Sherene. "More importantly, do *you* know what this means?" he asked her. "Our earlier conversation is even more significant now than ever."

*   *   *   *   *   *

Jamar was quick at making decisions. It was a trait he had acquired from his father. He had no trouble hearing someone's idea or even the facts about a case and rendering a speedy judgment. So it came as no surprise when early the next morning he told Shomo to have the army ready to move within a week. "Assemble all the officers for a strategy meeting at one o'clock this afternoon. I want everyone there so we can discuss *how* we'll take the mountain.

"Shomo, I also need a messenger to take this letter up to Lachish. Send me your fastest messenger as soon as possible."

*   *   *   *   *   *

As Ramiel and Sherene prepared to eat their lunch, one of the servants entered the room. "Excuse me Sire, but there is a man here who says he has a message for you."

"A message? For me? From whom?" Ramiel looked perplexed.

"He says it is a message from the King of Zarasitong."

Ramiel glanced at Sherene and then back to the servant. "Send him in."

A strong-looking young man, perhaps in his late teens or early twenties strode into the room. He glanced around at the surroundings and walked directly toward Ramiel. "This is for you." He extended his arm and handed Ramiel the letter he had received from Jamar a few hours earlier.

"Thank you," said Ramiel. The man stood still facing the king. "Is there something else?" Ramiel inquired.

"I am supposed to wait for a response, sir."

"Oh," responded the king. He thought for just a moment and then said, "Well, then I suppose you could wait outside while I read the letter and see if I have a response."

"Very well." The man turned on his heel and walked out.

Ramiel tore open the letter and read.

To the King of Lachish
From Jamar Leōn, King of Zarasitong

Our armies have conquered every kingdom in the region save yours. Asherese, Dunirk, Sudilin and Sudiner, Ustanol and the rest have all fallen before our powerful force. We are even now gathering at the foot of your mountain in preparation to bring you and your people under our domain. It will be useless to resist. We advise that you surrender now.

As a token that you and your people are laying down their arms and willingly surrendering, send us both your crown and the treasure from the top of the mountain. We will expect to receive these tributes within four days' time.

Ramiel reread the letter. He stared at it for awhile then looked at Sherene.

"What is it, Ramiel?" asked his wife. Sherene rose from her chair and walked over to her husband.

"Your brother wants to rule the entire region, including Lachish. He's asking us...no, he's telling us, to surrender."

Sherene took the letter and read it for herself. "Jamar was always impulsive as a little boy, too. He nearly always got what he wanted." Sherene smiled as she remembered little Jamar. "I would have thought he might have outgrown that."

"Apparently not," said Ramiel.

"Why don't we just tell him about the diary?"

asked Sherene.

"Of course," responded her husband. "Better yet, why don't we show him? We'll invite him to a special dinner and tell him we have a surprise that we think he'll find very interesting. At the dinner we can show him the diary. When he realizes that our people are all related he'll surely let us live in peace." Turning to one of the servants, Ramiel said, "Bring me paper, pen and the official seal."

The requested items were brought, and Ramiel wrote quickly. As he wrote, Sherene suggested, "Dear, maybe you could hint at the surprise by saying something like, 'Of course, we'll share all that we have, all our treasures, with you, our brothers.'"

"That's a brilliant idea, my love. That's sure to pique Jamar's interest."

"And maybe you should mention to him about the treasure," suggested Sherene.

"No. No, I think that should be a surprise also." Ramiel finished the letter, secured it with the official seal, and sent the messenger on his way.

*   *   *   *   *   *

Jamar looked at the letter. "Share?! Share the treasure? I don't want to share it. We'll take it all." He paused as he continued reading. "Hmmm. And a surprise, huh?" he said to no one in particular as he looked thoughtfully toward the mountain. "Maybe we'll just give him a little surprise of our own. Three days is not much time to prepare, though."

He turned back to the messenger. "Tell Shomo to assemble the officers immediately. All our plans have changed. Then return here first thing in the morning, because I will need you to carry another message to Lachish."

*   *   *   *   *   *

The atmosphere was tense as the officers sat around the large table.

"Are you sure this is what you want to do?" It was Shomo who inquired. None of the other officers had the nerve or the relationship with Jamar to question him like Shomo. "Technically this is your brother-in-law we're dealing with, you know."

Jamar didn't flinch a bit. "A brother-in-law I've never met...nor wanted," he responded angrily.

"And your sister will undoubtedly be at the dinner."

This caused Jamar to pause for just a moment. He replied thoughtfully, "We will try to be careful with Sherene. However, she made her choice years ago, and she will need to accept the consequences of her choice."

"I just want to make sure you've thought through the consequences yourself," said Shomo. Then he added, "It's not like you've never been impulsive before." Shomo smiled from ear to ear at Jamar. There were some nervous movements in the room until Jamar also broke into a smile.

"Yes, Shomo, my friend. I recognize the consequences from my side, also." Jamar looked around the room. "Gentlemen, since I was a boy I have dreamed about Lachish and the treasure. My father told me stories—as his father had told him stories—about a treasure so great no one could imagine. In my mind's eye I can almost see the vastness of the wealth. Everything else until now has been preliminary. It has all been simply preparation for this one conquest. We will take the mountain. We will possess the treasure." He paused to let his words sink in. "Now unless there is any further discussion about the overall idea, let's look at the specifics. Here's my plan...."

Dad stopped, put down the book, and smiled at his children.

"You can't stop there," complained Kyle. "What's the plan?"

"Hopefully we'll find out tomorrow night," said Dad. "Right now it's time to get this mess cleaned up."

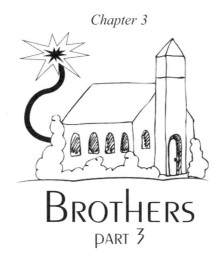

Chapter 3

Brothers
part 3

W ell, it looks like everything will probably come to a head tonight. The congregational meeting starts at 7:30. From what I can tell, we may have just enough votes to end this thing, but I'm not sure of anything yet. This meeting could get pretty nasty." Bill looked worried. "I can't figure out what some of those people are thinking. How can they defend this guy?"

"I know, dear. I'll sure be glad when it's all over," said Julie. "I just hope we still have a church left. This has been terrible on all of us." She paused. "I hope we're doing the right thing."

"The right thing?!" Bill looked startled. "Of course it's the right thing. You know we need someone new, someone who will take us further than we've been for the last *eight years*." Bill emphasized the last two words with a bit of disdain in his voice.

"Yes, of course. You're right." Julie looked thoughtful. "It's just that, well, some of the people we've been in relationship with for years don't see it quite the same way. Will we still be friends if...?" Her voice trailed off.

"Everything is going to be fine," said Bill.

"I hope so." Julie tried not to look worried as she glanced over toward the stove. "You'd better call the kids. Supper's ready."

*   *   *   *   *   *

"Kyle, if and when you get married, you'd better make sure she can cook like your mother. We're pretty spoiled here in this house. We don't know how well off we are. Not many folks today eat the kind of home cookin' your mom makes for us every night."

Julie smiled at her husband. "Well, thank you. I'm glad you liked it."

"And I believe it is the cook's turn to choose the Bible verse tonight."

Julie picked up the Bible card holder, and in her best imitation of Shelly, looked them over carefully. "Hmmmm...I can't decide..."

"Mo-om," Kyle complained, "just pick one."

She smiled. "I am, dear. Don't be in such a hurry." She pulled out a green card and looked at it. She frowned and stole a quick glance at her husband.

"What does it say?" he asked.

"It's from 1 Peter 4:8. 'Above all, love each other deeply.'" She repeated it, "*Above all*, love each other deeply."

Shelly's inquisitiveness got the best of her again. "Since it says, 'Above all,' does that mean that's *the* most important thing we should do?"

"Well, usually," answered her father.

"Then," began Shelly apprehensively, "when is loving each other not the most important thing?"

"Oh, there's lots of times, Shelly," responded her father gruffly. "I tell you what...let's find out what happens with Jamar. I think we'll finish the story tonight." Dad reached for the book, found the page where they had left off, and read.

Ramiel read the letter and then turned to Sherene. "He's accepted our offer. He will come with several of his officers two days from now. We must begin the preparations. I want everyone involved."

"Then I'm glad you made the decision to share with our people about the contents of the diary ahead of time," said Sherene. "Since they already understand what we are doing and why we are doing it, they will be more likely to pitch in and help."

"Moolan and Punker have already been making preliminary plans for the banquet. Now we will turn them loose to make it happen."

Sherene looked concerned. "There is a lot of work to do in a very short time. Are you sure *they* can handle it?"

The king smiled at his wife. "Moolan and Punker are certainly an odd-looking pair, but I'm sure they can handle the task. Let's get them going." He turned to a servant, "Skoon, summon Moolan and Punker for me right away."

"Yes, Sire."

*   *   *   *   *   *

"Is everything ready?" asked Jamar.

"Yes, Sire," replied a nearby officer. "Shomo and the soldiers have moved out and are in position. They will begin their ascent shortly after we do."

"Good. Then let's get started."

No one on the mountain had seen the soldiers making their way to the other side of the mountain during the night. Soldiers from as far away as Sudilin and Feronere and every place in between were part of the army. Enough soldiers remained in Zarasitong to make it look like a busy military camp, but they were just for show. The majority of the force had moved to the far side of Lachish mountain to prepare for the attack. After Jamar and his party started up the mountain, the army would move stealthily up the other side. They hoped the people of Lachish would be so involved in the festivities with the invited guests that no one would notice the great horde ascending from the opposite direction. They were right.

*   *   *   *   *   *

Jamar and company had their weapons with them. They were not sure when the "surprise" would come, but they were certain they knew what Ramiel and the people of Lachish had planned for them. Jamar had repeatedly cautioned his men to "be ready for anything." They were.

Ramiel greeted the visitors with overwhelming warmth and friendliness. The words that were spoken—seemingly in sincerity—, the gifts that were bestowed, the lavishness of the banquet laid out for them, all caused Jamar to wonder. Then he saw Sherene, his sister whom he had not seen in years. She came to Jamar and hugged him. She had tears in her eyes. They spoke briefly, but then Ramiel interrupted. Sherene promised that they would talk more later.

Something continued to gnaw at the inside of Jamar. *Either these folks are putting on an amazing acting job or...* No, he wouldn't allow himself to choose the other choice. He couldn't have been wrong. Certainly not that wrong. He decided that at any moment the people of Lachish would attack, and he must keep his mind focused on that. To allow himself the luxury of liking these people would be a major tactical error. *That's what they want us to do*, he thought. *Then just when we are totally at ease, they'll pounce.*

The banquet began, and the abundance of food overwhelmed the people from Zarasitong. They were served more varieties of food than any of them had ever seen at one meal. Even Jamar had never seen the likes of a feast like this.

In the midst of the lavish spread, Jamar knew he was beginning to lose some of his officers. They were being won over by the kindness and generosity of the people of Lachish. He also knew that at any moment they would hear the sound of the trumpet signaling Shomo's attack.

For about a half of a second Jamar thought about running out of the great hall to find Shomo and stop the attack. Then he realized that this would surely be suicide for him and his men. No, they would go forward as planned.

Jamar nonchalantly rose from the table and quickly went around the room talking with people. To each of his own men he whispered a simple command, "Stay focused. Stay with the plan." His words seemed to have the desired effect. The men had a different attitude after he spoke with them. They were ready for the battle.

Just as Ramiel stood to address the crowd, a great trumpet blast was heard from outside. None of those in the banqueting hall had time to do anything. Jamar's men had been specially chosen because of their speed and ability with their weapons. All of the men of Lachish who were in the room lay dead in a matter of moments. From the noises outside, the battle did not last long there either. *It was almost too fast*, thought Jamar, *almost as though they were completely unprepared to fight*. Again, however, Jamar did not allow his thoughts to go in that direction. Instead he yelled, "To the treasure!"

From the other side of the great hall a woman's voice called weakly, "Wait!" It was Sherene. She had been wounded in the battle. Her left shoulder was bleeding profusely, and she leaned on a chair to support herself. In her free hand she held a leather-bound book. "Jamar...why?" she cried. She paused and stared at her brother. "Ramiel was about to show you this." Awkwardly because of her wound, she held up the book. "This is a diary that shows that Lachish and Zarasitong were brothers." Sherene paused again, obviously becoming weaker by the moment. "They came to this area...to seek a new life...Once they got here...they separated." She coughed. "Lachish chose the mountain and... Zarasitong, the valley." Sherene slowly lowered herself to sit on the chair on which she had been leaning. She laid the diary on the table. "Jamar, the people of Zarasitong and the people of Lachish... are brothers. Why...why have you murdered your own relatives?" Sherene wept. Then she looked up from her tears, and although words were becoming more difficult she gasped, "Was it...the treasure, Jamar? Is that...what...you wanted? If so, go...get it...because you...deserve it now." Then she collapsed onto the table.

Jamar ran to his sister. He instinctively felt her pulse, but he knew there would be none. It was too late. Jamar picked up the diary and turned a few pages. He read some and flipped a few more pages. Though he had not read the entire volume, he had seen enough to give credibility to what Sherene had said. One last time, though, he refused to believe that he had made a mistake. They had come for the treasure. They were going to have it. After all, he reasoned, his sister told him in her dying breath that he deserved it. It was time. Jamar walked slowly out of the room, followed by his loyal men.

Outside, the carnage was worse than they had seen inside. Bodies were strewn everywhere. The street was nearly red with blood. The men had taken no prisoners, and they left no survivors.

As her husband read, Julie suddenly saw a picture in her mind. All of their friends from church were in the fellowship hall...and they were screaming at one another. Close friends lay on the floor and slumped over tables, bleeding and wounded. Their words were piercing one another like swords. The carnage was terrible. The picture nearly overwhelmed Julie. She trembled at the sight.

Jamar and company solemnly walked up about three hundred yards to a huge boulder at the top of the mountain. Of course, this detail—like all the other details of Jamar's army—was already planned. Four men with the necessary equipment stepped forward to move the rock. Just as quickly, the boulder was rolled away, and Jamar moved close to see what lay beneath.

As his eyes adjusted to the darkness of the hole, Jamar realized that there was no brimming treasure chest. There were no diamonds or jewels. No gold or silver. All he saw was simply a polished stone, something like a small tombstone, that read:

The last words given to us by our father:
LOVE ONE ANOTHER

Jamar looked frantically around at those gathered there, and then back at the stone. He read it and reread it. Then his face twisted into a look of agony and he lifted his gaze toward the sky. He closed his eyes and shouted at the top of his voice, "NO-O-O-O!" As the sound of his voice subsided, Jamar fell to his knees and wept.

Bill Spencer closed the book and gently laid it on the table. It was clearly not the ending he had expected. When he looked up, tears streamed down Julie's face. She was staring at the Bible verse she still clutched in her hand, and she kept repeating the words, "Above all. *Above all*."

Chapter 4

LOVE ONE ANOTHER

The final words given by the father of Lachish and Zarasitong were a command, "Love one another." Similarly, on His final night before going to the cross, Jesus said, "A new command I give you: *Love one another.* As I have loved you, so you must *love one another.* By this shall all men know that you are my disciples, if you *love one another*" (John 13:34-35). Three times in fewer than thirty Greek words Jesus says, "Love one another." Truly loving one another is indeed, as Jamar's father had told him, a treasure beyond imagination.

Jesus' words in this section of Scripture are in the context of His final Passover meal. Jesus was right in the middle of telling His disciples that He was going to a place where they couldn't come. Peter—impetuous Peter—spoke up and declared that he would follow Jesus anywhere. "I will lay down my life for you," said Peter. But Jesus told him, "Before the rooster crows, you will disown me three times."

Jesus knew that Peter was going to deny Him. This was not even slightly a surprise to Jesus. He was quite aware of the fact that Peter would disown Him, denying he even knew Him. But Jesus chose to love him anyway.

This is the context where Jesus tells us to have the same kind of love for each other. Three times He tells His followers, "Love one another." Even in the midst of failure, love one another. When someone messes up, love one another. When your brother stumbles and falls, love one another.

Do you recall when the women went to the tomb on Easter morning? They found an angel there. Do you remember the angel's words? "Go tell His disciples *and Peter*..." (Mark 16:7).

Doesn't that seem a little odd? After all, Peter *was* one of Jesus' disciples. Why did the angel emphasize Peter's name? Why single out his name and none of the others? I get the impression that Jesus was letting Peter know he was still accepted. "I know you blew it, Peter, but I still love you."

Apparently Peter thoroughly understood the lesson. He seems to have grasped the love and acceptance that Jesus offered. That's why years later when he wrote letters to God's people, he could say, "*Above all*, love each other deeply" (1 Peter 4:8). Jesus' clear love and acceptance of him caused Peter to want to pass that lesson on to others.

It is interesting to note that the Lord doesn't seem to allow any leniency because of our personalities, or even things like our political views. He still insists that we love one another. Two of Jesus' hand-picked disciples, Simon the Zealot and Matthew the tax collector, were about as opposite as you could get in that society. The Zealots were pro-Israel in every sense of the word. They wanted to battle the Romans and drive those uncircumcised heathen from their land. The tax collectors, on the other hand, had, in essence, sold out to the Romans. Their job was to collect taxes from their fellow-Hebrews and give the money to Rome. In Israel, Zealots and tax collectors were polar opposites. Picture an ultra-conservative Republican sitting next to a passionate, far-left-wing Democrat. Ideologically, they were as far apart as possible. Yet, both of those guys, Simon and Matthew, were right there with the rest at the final Passover meal when Jesus gave His disciples the thrice-repeated message: love one another.

The truth is, though, that our natural inclination appears to go in the opposite direction. Too often we act like terrorists, slashing one another with our words and deeds. If we disagree with someone we have a tendency to villainize that person. Jesus, however, told us to love one another. Period.

Popular author T. Davis Bunn has a unique way of weaving historical facts into his fictional novels. In one scene from his book, *The Amber Room*, Herr Diehl is giving a tour of Erfurt, Germany. From the town marketplace they climb a broad staircase that is nearly three hundred feet high. At the top are two very large old cathedrals.

"The first is the one on the left," Herr Diehl told them as they climbed. "It was erected in 1154 as a monastery and remained true to the faith, so the story goes, through kingdoms and centuries. During the Reformation, the monks ridiculed the Pope's political ambitions and refused to back his demands for a war against their Protestant brethren. In reply, the Pope commanded that a second church be built, close enough and big enough to dominate the original."

One church alone would have been majestic. The two together looked ridiculous. Both were vast structures whose spires reached heavenward several hundred feet. Vast swatches of stained-glass windows arched between flanking buttresses of stone and dark-stained mortar. Nearby four-story buildings were easily dwarfed by the twin churches.

"And so stands a warning to the church of today," Herr Diehl said. "A witness to what can happen when doctrine becomes more important than the straightforward laws of love given us by a simple Carpenter. Whenever one of us opens our mouth to condemn the way another worships, we set another brick in the wall of such a monstrosity.

We offer our beloved Savior up to the nonbelievers as a point of ridicule. If we as the saved cannot agree to disagree in peace and love and brotherhood, what do we show the nonbelievers but the same discord and disharmony from which they seek to escape?"[1]

Jesus was not ambiguous when He said, "Love one another." This was not a suggestion, nor even an emergency, stopgap command. This was *the* command for Jesus' followers. "By this shall all men know that you are my disciples, if you love one another." There is no way to misinterpret those words. Far more than our doctrinal agreement, eloquent speech or kind deeds toward outsiders, the fact that we love each other should identify us as followers of Jesus. Without question, our love for one another is to be the identifying mark of the Church. And in order to be that identifying mark, love must be visibly demonstrated toward one another.

Inquisitive little Shelly asked her father, "When is loving one another not the most important thing?" Though we don't always obey this command, the truth is that *is always* the most important thing.

Chapter 5

God's Perspective

Sam and Alice were relatively new at the church. They had come from another local church that had recently gone through some very turbulent times. Friendly, articulate and outgoing, Sam and Alice had quickly established themselves as leaders in their new congregation. Eventually, though, their friendliness toward some had worn off.

Andrew Wright received an angry phone call after a committee meeting one night. Sam soundly denounced

Andrew's opinions about the church's upcoming anniversary celebration and suggested he should stick to areas where he was more gifted. Sam wanted God's work to be as potent as possible, and that meant the right people should be in the right places. Andrew, a long-standing but shy member at the church, resigned from the committee.

Shirley and Jan encountered Alice's wrath after a morning Bible study meeting. She didn't agree with their thoughts on the Holy Spirit's role in the Church today. She informed them that she had done a great deal of study and research on the subject and, unless they were prepared for a full public debate, next time they should keep their ideas on the subject to themselves. Alice honestly desired pure doctrine with no dross. The result was that she silenced two Christian women from ever speaking up in their Bible study again. Ever.

As it turned out, these two incidents were just the tip of the iceberg. Alice and Sam unwittingly pitted old friends against one another. They wormed their way into the hearts of some—those they considered to be walking closely with the Lord—while intentionally alienating others who just didn't measure up to their standards. It didn't take long before the internal strife reached a fever pitch.

It was discovered too late that Alice and Sam were at the forefront of the problems in their previous church.

I wish I could tell you that this story is entirely fictional like the one at the beginning of this book. Unfortunately, it's not. It is actually a combination of two different scenarios I recently encountered. Two true stories that have been multiplied many times over in churches all around the world.

Too frequently, rather than showing love, we have a tendency to sow seeds of dissension. Perhaps we view divisiveness as acceptable because it is all around us. We regularly see politicians fighting among themselves, union workers arguing with management, environmentalists feuding with industry. All of these and more are a routine part of our society. When we see this type of activity, we generally view it as normal. From God's perspective, however, it is not normal, especially in the Church.

Although God is love, the Bible makes it clear that there are some things He hates. The Lord hates, among other things, "a man who stirs up dissension among brothers" (see Proverbs 6:16-19). You might be thinking, "So what? God hating someone who stirs up dissension isn't that big of deal, is it?"

It is, if you truly understand the character of God. The Lord never does anything half-heartedly. Everything He does is filled with zeal and with passion. Consider the fact that His love is so all-encompassing that He gave up His only Son for the sake of the people He created. The Bible often refers to "the zeal of the Lord." God's zeal is a major part of His character. He never does anything with only partial feeling. Everything the Lord does is full of fervor and passion.

In light of this, what must God's hatred be like? He obviously is not opposed to using violence toward those who cross Him. Ask Egypt's Pharaoh about the destructive plagues that consumed his nation because he refused to obey the Lord. Ask Uzzah—who touched the Ark of the Covenant and died as a result—about God's severity. Ask the Israelites about the repeated warnings they ignored and the ultimate calamities—even death and slavery—that resulted. The Bible is replete with stories of those who died or were severely disciplined because they went against the clearly delineated will of God.

Death. Plagues. Slavery. Just because they didn't do what the Lord said? I don't know about you, but I want to stay as far away from God's hatred as I can. Suddenly, the Lord hating someone who stirs up dissension does sound like a really big deal, doesn't it?

Unfortunately, our perspective doesn't always line up with God's. We don't usually think that being divisive is so bad. In reality we have a tendency to rate sins like events at the Olympics are rated. We would most likely rate adultery at least a 9.5. We would probably see embezzling funds from the church as being a perfect 10. You can't get any higher than that. However, disunity, from our usual perspective, is probably only about a 2 or maybe a 3. It really doesn't seem all that bad to us. God's Word shows us that this kind of thinking is badly flawed.

Galatians 5:19–21 lists the "acts of the sinful nature." The list consists of things like "sexual immorality," "idolatry," "witchcraft," "hatred," etc. All of these things are sins we would expect to be there. Each of these is dreadful and obviously needs to be on the list, even from our perspective. Although there may have been times in our lives when we have participated in any one or more of these, we know they are wrong. However, also included in this sinful nature list are things like "discord," "dissensions," and "factions." These things, that to us seem like no big deal, are just as heinous to the Lord as the others.

God does not use our sin rating system. To Him, sin is sin. "For whoever keeps the whole law and yet stumbles at just one point is guilty of breaking all of it" (James 2:10). Even though from God's perspective all sin is the same, the damaging effects sin has in people's lives may vary. The problem with disunity is that the effects are often subtle and frequently go unnoticed and uncorrected.

Pastor Norman Willis articulated it well when he said, "Far worse than any sex scandal or financial misappropriation is the scandal of disunity facing the Body of Christ. The insidiousness of this scandal is that it has become acceptable in Christian circles and in some churches, elevated to an art form."[1]

In his wonderful book, *Love in Action*, Robert Moeller had this to say, "We claim something that no other religion in the world claims—that God Himself makes His home in our lives. That's why ugly and nasty infighting reflects not only on ourselves, but on the character of God."[2]

Like Sam and Alice, and also like Bill Spencer and company in our opening story, some Christians think they are being helpful when they stir up dissension. The reality is, though, that this is as far from the truth as heaven is from hell. They are unwittingly becoming terrorists. We must recognize that being divisive is not an option. God hates it, and it is destroying the strength of the Body of Christ.

Chapter 6

WHATEVER YOU DID FOR ONE OF THE LEAST OF THESE...

Of course the opening story of this book is fictional. However, it could very well be true. The events are really not too far-fetched. Actually, these are common scenes in many families and many churches. How often have you or I said or done things to our brothers and sisters in Christ which we later deeply regretted? How often have we been terrorists in our own churches?

Several times the Bible refers to the Church as "the Body of Christ." Since we are indeed a body we should act like a body. Would your brain ever intentionally cause your hand to cut off your toes? Or purposefully and forcefully smash your face into a brick wall? Of course not. Yet we perpetrate these types of afflictions on the spiritual Body—the Body of Christ—on a regular basis with seemingly very little thought given to the consequences.

In the book of Acts we are first introduced to a man named Saul of Tarsus. Saul later becomes Paul the apostle, but his first mention is at the stoning of Stephen. The anti-Christian people were stoning Stephen because of his perceived blasphemy. Scripture says, "Meanwhile, the witnesses laid their clothes at the feet of a young man named Saul" (Acts 7:58).

A couple of verses later we read these words about Saul of Tarsus: "And Saul was there, giving approval to his death. On that day a great persecution broke out against the church at Jerusalem, and all except the apostles were scattered throughout Judea and Samaria" (Acts 8:1).

Two more verses down there is more. "But Saul began to destroy the church. Going from house to house, he dragged off men and women and put them in prison" (Acts 8:3).

Then, finally, in the next chapter there is even further information about Saul. "Meanwhile, Saul was still breathing out murderous threats against the Lord's disciples. He went to the high priest and asked him for letters to the synagogues in Damascus, so that if he found any there who belonged to the Way, whether men or women, he might take them as prisoners to Jerusalem" (Acts 9:1-2).

Saul of Tarsus was not an especially nice guy. If you were a Christian he was not the man you wanted your daughter bringing home to talk about their marriage intentions. In this place and time Saul was the number one human enemy of the Church. However, Saul soon had an encounter of a different kind.

> As he neared Damascus on his journey, suddenly a light from heaven flashed around him. He fell to the ground and heard a voice say to him, "Saul, Saul, why do you persecute me?"
>
> "Who are you, Lord?" Saul asked.
>
> "I am Jesus, whom you are persecuting," he replied...
>
> Saul got up from the ground, but when he opened his eyes he could see nothing. (Acts 9:3-5, 8a).

Please recognize that there is no indication that Saul could see anything from the time the bright light flashed until three days later when Ananias prayed for him and "something like scales" fell from his eyes. Try to picture this scenario in your mind. The bright light flashes and Saul falls to the ground. He hears a voice ask him why he is persecuting the person, but he can't see anyone or anything.

In Saul's mind, he was probably thinking, "Oh my. Is

this someone—maybe Stephen—coming back from the dead to haunt me? Or perhaps it's someone who I've been tracking." Therefore Saul says, "Who are you, Lord?"

In the Greek, the word "Lord" does not necessarily mean *the* Lord. It is often simply a term of respect. We would liken it to our word, "sir." "Who are you, Lord?" Saul asked. "Who are you, sir?"

Then comes a most unexpected response. "I am Jesus, whom you are persecuting."

At this point Saul could have easily and accurately responded, "Jesus?! I never even met you." Quite possibly Saul never even saw Jesus during His earthly ministry.

More importantly, though, think about the ramifications of that phrase, "I am Jesus, whom you are persecuting." Saul wasn't actually persecuting Jesus, just His followers.

However, from Jesus' perspective, clearly it was more than that. The Lord has so tied Himself to His people that we become one with Him. When someone does something to us as the Church, it is as though they are doing it to Jesus Himself.

Jesus said much the same thing when He talked about His return.

> Then the King will say to those on his right, "Come, you who are blessed by my Father; take your inheritance, the kingdom prepared for you since the creation of the world. For I was hungry and you gave me something to eat, I was thirsty and you gave me something to drink, I was a stranger

and you invited me in, I needed clothes and you clothed me, I was sick and you looked after me, I was in prison and you came to visit me."

Then the righteous will answer him, "Lord, when did we see you hungry and feed you, or thirsty and give you something to drink? When did we see you a stranger and invite you in, or needing clothes and clothe you? When did we see you sick or in prison and go to visit you?"

The King will reply, "I tell you the truth, *whatever you did for one of the least of these brothers of mine, you did for me*" (Matthew 25:34-40).

This is the positive version of the same principle. When someone does something to one of God's people, it is as though they are doing it to God Himself. "Whatever you did for one of the least of these brothers of mine, *you did for me*."

Jesus reiterated this idea in a slightly different way when He said, "I tell you the truth, whoever accepts anyone I send accepts me; and whoever accepts me accepts the one who sent me" (John 13:20). As His people, we are more than just the *representation* of Christ here on earth. We are, in reality, His Body.

When Jesus asked why Saul was persecuting Him, he meant it. Saul was not simply antagonizing and killing Jesus' followers. From Jesus' perspective, the persecution was directed toward Him.

Let's take this a step further and make this personal.

This is not just about outsiders doing something to one of us. This is not only a matter of non-Christians doing nasty things to Christians. When Jesus was talking in the Matthew passage above, He was referring to "the righteous" (i.e., believers, Christians). Those people did kind deeds for "the least of these brothers of mine," and the king said, "You did it for me." Again, this is the positive aspect, but there is a negative side also. When we in the Body of Christ do mean-spirited things toward one another, it is as though we have done those things to Jesus Himself.

Sometimes we embark on what we perceive to be a mission from God. We see someone in the Body of Christ who we believe is in error, so we endeavor to right the situation. When we do this, we often end up being terrorists. Though we believe we are doing something that is ultimately for the other person's good, we don't realize how horrendously destructive are our actions.

You know what? That's exactly what Saul of Tarsus did. He was certain he was right in his persecutions. He was a Pharisee, one of the truly righteous folks. In his mind his actions were completely justified. He was right and they were wrong. But then Jesus told him otherwise.

Have you ever defended your words or actions like this? "I know I said some rather unkind things about Mary, but they were all true." So? True or not, your words may well have brought injury to your own spiritual body. You may have persecuted and injured Christ.

Saul of Tarsus was certain he was right in persecuting

Christians—and his conviction was based on Scripture. However, he had obviously missed God's heart. He was following the letter of the law and missed the spirit of it. He ignored the mercy and unfailing love of God.

In his book, *Soul Survivor*, Philip Yancey explains that the church in which he grew up was very legalistic and harsh. Many times over the years he has lamented ever being affiliated with that church. The things he saw and the treatment he received left a lasting negative impression. However, Yancey says this about his reaction:

> What is my snobbishness toward my childhood church, for instance, but an inverted form of the harsh judgment it showed me? Whenever faith seems an entitlement, or a measuring rod, we cast our lots with the Pharisees and grace softly slips away.[1]

He's right. Most of the time when we believe we are more correct than a fellow-Christian, we express that belief in a judgmental way. In doing so, we are ignoring the fact that we are—together, collectively—the Body of Christ.

Augustine wrote these words concerning our being Christ's Body, "Let us rejoice then and give thanks that we are made not only Christians, but Christ. Do you understand brethren and apprehend the grace of God upon us? Marvel, be glad, we are made Christ. For He is the head, we are the members: the whole man is He and we!"

Now, don't begin to think that I've gone new-agish and am proclaiming that somehow we become little gods. Nothing could be further from the truth. However, if we are indeed the Body of Christ then somehow we are joined to Him, the Head.

Jesus used a different analogy when He talked about Himself as the Vine and us as the branches (John 15:5). Have you ever pruned a branch from a tree? It is impossible to tell *exactly* where the trunk of the tree ends and the branch begins. There is an intermixing that happens at the point of connection. The same is true in our relationship with Christ. We are somehow so joined to Him that we become part of Him.

In light of this, it is regrettable that many Christians apparently fail to recognize that since we are indeed the *Body* of Christ we should act like a body. Your head would never tell your hand to tear off your nose. The Lord doesn't command these kinds of actions either. He does not direct the foot to kick the stomach. He would never lead one person to go against His Word by gossiping about or assaulting the character of another. God does not authorize "terrorist activity" within His own Body.

Unfortunately, just like Kyle assaulting the character of Jane, his cancer-stricken acquaintance, or Julie Spencer sharing the news (translated: gossip) from her friend about Pastor Wallace's late night activities, we too often assault others with our words. Those kinds of things happen quite regularly in the Church today, and when they happen, we are clearly not acting like the *Body* of Christ.

How about a practical suggestion? The next time you

find yourself saying something that you shouldn't about a brother or sister in Christ, try this: slap yourself across the face or punch your arm or leg. And I'm not talking about just a little love tap. Do it hard. Make it hurt. Why? Because that's the same thing you're doing to the Body of Christ with unkind words.

We need to recognize that we are—together—the Body of Christ. "Now you are the body of Christ, and *each one of you is a part of it*" (1 Corinthians 12:27)

Chapter 7

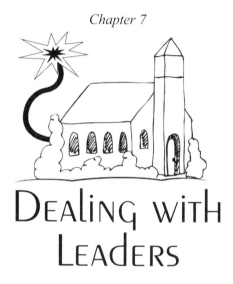

DEALING WITH
LEADERS

It is clear that God's people have seemingly always found fault with one another, especially with leaders. Although we really don't know the thought process of Judas Iscariot, it seems obvious that he found enough fault with Jesus to betray Him. Jesus! The holy Son of God! If someone close—someone who was consistently with Him and knew His heart—found fault with Him, it should be pretty easy to find fault with the rest of us.

In our opening story, Bill Spencer had found enough offense in Pastor Wallace's actions to want to get rid of him. Although the reasons certainly had no scriptural basis, nonetheless Spencer was willing to lead the charge for his removal. Let's look at this scenario for a moment.

Spencer noted that Pastor Wallace had been at the church for eight years and the congregation had not really grown in numbers in that time. So? Is that a reason to oust him? Where in the Bible does it guarantee that a church should grow by a certain percentage in a certain amount of time? More significantly, where does Scripture proclaim that if that increase is not attained, that it is solely the fault of the pastor? Clearly Spencer's plan to remove Pastor Wallace has no honest basis from God's Word. In spite of that fact, an offense has been taken and now any other minor infraction, real or perceived, simply adds fuel to the fire. Kyle's assertion that their pastor is not as good at preaching as the pastor at another church reinforces his father's convictions.

Further, Spencer hears that his wife's friend, Ramona Heinz, has seen Pastor Wallace leaving the Rodriguez's home by himself late at night. With the recognition that Mr. Rodriguez is absent, Spencer's mind jumps to what for him, in light of everything else, is an obvious conclusion. No matter that Mrs. Rodriguez had invited the pastor and his wife to come over and pray because of a rebel uprising in the Central American country where her husband was working. No matter that Pastor Wallace walked out the door of the house just as Ramona drove past. No matter that the pastor's wife lingered inside a few moments longer giving comfort to a very worried wife. In the midst of the offense, a conclusion was drawn. The accusation was carefully aimed and fired. The verdict rendered: guilty. Terrorists had stealthily snuck in and done their devastating damage.

It is a common line of thought that the end justifies the means. This ideology says that the end result makes our actions in getting to those end results acceptable. If we get a better pastor out of this situation and that helps the church, what difference does it make how that comes about?

One day a friend of mine made a suggestion regarding this philosophy that I had never considered before. He said, "Perhaps—just perhaps—all we have are the means." What he was saying is that over time our goals may change. The end results we think we want now may not be the same ones we want to reach twenty years from now. Instead, the higher motivation is handling the situations we encounter in a God-honoring way. We must throw out the end-justifies-the-means mentality and handle each situation in accordance with the precepts of God's Word.

I have frequently seen situations where congregational members were addressing what they perceived as faulty leadership. Regrettably, the tactics used by the followers were far more abusive and ungodly than any leader ever could have been. Although certainly there are situations of heavy-handed or even abusive leadership in churches, my experience has been that those are rare compared with the abuse measured out by the "followers."

I have witnessed situations where a pastor was seriously and viciously maligned for being disorganized. I've encountered other times when congregation members have started an insurrection against the pastor because he either didn't visit every member at least once per year or didn't visit every member who became hospitalized. There was also the pastor who was asked to leave because he dared to use a different version of the Bible than the one that had been used for years in their congregation. Please note that not one of these situations was because of a clear biblical mandate. Each one was a personal preference issue.

Most people, when they believe that a leader is in error, are not honestly interested in correction. They want what they perceive to be justice (regardless of whether that "justice" has any basis in Scripture). No matter what scriptural injunctions (such as love, gentleness and kindness) are thrown to the wind, they are "right" and will do absolutely anything and everything to prove it—including violating clear sections of God's Word. These are clearly terrorist activities.

In his fictional book *Avalon*, popular author Stephen Lawhead creates this scene that helps make the point.

> "You know," said the Archbishop after a moment, "people assume a churchman's life is dull as dishwater, that we glide blissfully from one placid appointment to the next with nothing more exciting that the occasional homily to liven our luxuriously empty days."

"What?" James asked in feigned surprise. "You mean it's not like that?"

"Not by a long shot," Rippon declared with a flat chop of his hand. "I'm here to tell you it's a snake pit—worse than that even. Most reptiles only strike in self-defense, but our variety bite for the sheer joy of inflicting pain...It's war, but without the blood and bombs. When I was a lad in Berkshire, I used to dream of one day commanding a fighting ship on the high seas. God certainly has a wicked sense of humor, because my ambition has been fulfilled in spades. The only difference between an archbishop and an admiral is that an admiral in the Royal Navy doesn't have to engage in daily hand-to-hand combat with his own shipmates."[1]

One need not be an archbishop to experience the same scenario. Practically anyone who has ever been in ministry can echo those words. I don't know what kind of ministry background Lawhead has, but he certainly sounds as though he is speaking from experience. His words paint quite an accurate picture. How sad. What a contrast this is to the call Christ issued for us to truly and unconditionally love one another. Shouldn't our faithful—though human—leaders receive that love and respect instead of criticism, blame and our most subversive terrorist activities?

Please understand that there is a time to confront leadership. If you honestly believe they are acting contrary to

Scripture (very different from someone doing something you don't like), then it is time to speak up. However, even this must be done individually (not as a group or with a petition) in a humble, gentle, loving manner, sharing your perspective and listening to theirs. If, after such a meeting, you are unsatisfied with the results, you have two major options:

1. Stay, keep dialoguing, and trust that God will change either you or the leadership.
2. Leave.

In either case, pray that God will have His way in the situation. (That's very different from Him having *your* way.) In either case, you must not gossip or rally others around your cause. In either case, you must act in complete integrity, walking in love, humility, kindness, gentleness, mercy and forgiveness. Remember, Jesus is our example. When He was being crucified, He said, "Father, forgive them..." Even though He was completely innocent and they were completely wrong, He didn't lash out in retaliation.

The usual scenario is that the leadership does something with which someone does not agree. As a result, the person(s) either starts an insurrection against the leadership or leaves the church. Either way, they involve as many people with them as they can.

Unquestionably, one of the areas most prone to a lack of mercy and love in the Church is follower toward leader. Just like in the opening story, there are frequently perceptions of wrongdoing or ineptitude. Whatever the supposed offense, people go to any length to see it corrected. They willingly allow themselves to become terrorists in the Church. In that mode, if they don't stage a rebellion, the other common option is to exit in disgust, leaving a wake of negative comments—landmines waiting to wreak destruction—behind. We'll explore that scenario and its consequences in the next chapter.

If you have an issue of contention with the leadership of your church, I am not suggesting that you ignore it. You may well need to go and talk with your leader(s). It may even take more than one meeting. Beforehand, though, be honest with yourself. Is this a clear issue of Scripture or is it simply a personal preference? The answer to that question will make a big difference in how you proceed. In the entire process, if you really want to follow God's path, you must not be haughty and arrogant, but instead humble and gentle.

Chapter 8

COMMITMENT TO CHURCH

There was a man stranded on a deserted island for a very long time. One day a small ship was passing near the island. The man quickly ran to the beach and signaled for the boat to rescue him. The ship came in near to the shore and the captain called to the man, "Get everyone together because we must leave quickly. There is a major storm approaching, and we can not stay here."

The man on the island assured the captain that he was

the only one there.

"Then why are there three huts?" inquired the captain.

The man laughed as he responded. "Well, that one way over there is my house. And this one here is my church. And that one over there is the church I used to attend."

This guy couldn't even agree with himself!

People leaving churches in a disgruntled manner is almost epidemic today. When I mention to people that my wife and I have been a part of the same church for more than 25 years, they are almost always amazed. I think that's sad. We should not be the oddball because we've stayed for that long. From an honest biblical perspective, that should be the norm. Unfortunately, it isn't.[1]

Focus on the Family has a weekly faxed publication called *The Pastor's Weekly Briefing*. Some time ago this short excerpt caught my attention.

> A recent Barna survey discovered that 11% of those who attend a Christian church at least once a month plan to change their place of worship in the coming year. Barna said this, "Despite their fascination with spirituality, most church people are only moderately devoted to their current church and they are not deeply invested in spiritual growth." H.B. London, Jr. of Focus on the Family made this comment: "We, like trendy teenagers, seem to 'go where the action is'—follow the latest fad. We are a 'disposable society'—less inclined to loyalty."[2]

When faced with an uncomfortable situation, most people find it much easier to run than to stay and work it through in a godly fashion. Pastor John Bevere learned a valuable lesson about this early in his ministry.

> I will never forget the time a friend counseled me not to walk away from a very frustrating situation. "John, I know you can find scriptural reasons for walking away. Before you do that, make sure you have fought this in prayer and done all you can to bring the peace of God into this situation."
>
> Then he added, "You will regret it if you look back one day and ask yourself if you did all you could to save this relationship. It is better to know that you have no other recourse and that you did as much as possible without compromising truth."[3]

His friend's advice was accurate. I cannot count the number of people I have encountered in my travels who have told me that they left a church in an attitude of animosity and even rebellion. Very often they have expressed remorse for not staying and walking through the situation in a godly manner.

Perhaps the greater dilemma is that once you've left a church over a disagreement, it then becomes easier to leave the next time you're disgruntled. Instead of honestly working through differences, it is much easier to jump ship and go somewhere else. Although I would certainly not put commitment to a specific congregation on the same level as commitment to marriage, there are parallels. Statistics show that those who have divorced once are much more likely to do it again. The same is true in our congregational relationships. Leaving a church because of a disagreement makes it easier to leave the next time.

Popular author and pastor Joshua Harris recently wrote a book entitled *Stop Dating the Church*. In it, he says this:

> Going away is easy. Do you want to know what's harder? Do you want to know what takes more courage and what will make you grow faster than anything else? Join a local church and lay down your selfish desires by considering others more important than yourself. Humble yourself and acknowledge that you need other Christians. Invite them into your life. Stop complaining about what's wrong with the church, and become part of a solution.[4]

I'd like to suggest Christians running away from difficult situations is rare, but I wouldn't be honest if I did. I've witnessed the scene played over and over again in the lives of believers all across North America. People repeatedly run from uncomfortable situations and end up greatly hindered in their own spiritual walk.

Christians often have the notion that as long as they have Jesus they don't need the Church. In his excellent book, *Building High Commitment in a Low Commitment World*, Bill Hull addresses this issue.

Christian faith without commitment to the church is inferior Christianity. It is not normal for a Christian to live outside accountability to others and service in the church (Matthew 28:20; Ephesians 5:21; 1 Thessalonians 5:14; 1 Peter 4:10-11).[5]

Look at it this way. In a dead body, unity is missing. There is no head directing the functions; none of the various parts are working together. Each member pursues its own natural end—corruption and decay. In the human body, no member can live and grow unless it is joined to the rest of the body. Likewise, union with the Body of Christ is indispensable. We cannot ignore the necessity of our relationship with one another and still honestly live out our relationship with Christ.

Imagine a beautiful, ornate temple. Everything about it is lovely except that there is an oddly shaped hole in the wall where a stone is missing. If and when we realize that the hole is our spot, our natural tendency is to go in and knock the edges off nearby stones trying to make the shape fit us. Perhaps a better idea is to allow the Lord to knock the rough edges off us so that we will fit into *His* wall.

I teach seminars at churches across North America. My favorite seminar to teach is on the topic of unity and relationships. When I began developing the seminar I asked a friend who is very good at facilitating small group discussion to write some questions that would stimulate interaction. The questions he came up with are very thought-provoking. One in particular gives me pause each time I read it.

> To the extent that we shop for churches to suit our tastes, how much of this is out of a desire to protect our own sense of safety and comfort and meet our own needs (and avoid the hard work of growing into mature Christians who can demonstrate the difference between unity and conformity) and how much is out of a deep conviction that the Lord Himself is placing us right where He wants us?

Wow! This is a question that would be pretty tough for many Christians to answer honestly. It is much easier to "avoid the hard work of growing into mature Christians" than it is to trust that God placed us where He wants us. After all, if the Lord really did put us here, then we need to choose to grow together with our brothers and sisters in Christ. That's hard. It's much easier to run when conflict develops. That is not God's best, however.

I mentioned earlier that my wife and I have been a part of the same church for over 25 years. During that more than quarter-century there have been times when I have disagreed with the leadership of the church. There have been times when my wife and I didn't like some of the things that were happening in the church. Please understand that none of these situations were clearly unscriptural. In retrospect, they have all been opinion-based disagreements. However, there have even been times when I have entertained the thought of leaving because of these situations. I was not comfortable and getting out seemed like a viable option. But I didn't do it. Why not? Because my wife and I are convinced that the Lord, in His sovereignty and mercy, brought us to our specific congregation, and until He leads us on we're staying.

Leaving a church quietly and calmly is not necessarily a wrong thing to do. Most people, however, don't leave quietly or calmly. Like terrorists placing landmines in the paths of others, they let anyone and everyone who will listen know what they think, why they are offended and why they are leaving. Their words and actions will affect not only themselves but others also. The accusations made about leaders will not simply stop with the person making the accusation. Others will become tainted also.

Our opening story showed dialogue only among the Spencer family. Only a couple of other specific names were mentioned, Jim Crandall and Ramona Heinz, but apparently much of the church was somehow involved in the dispute on one side or the other. Harsh words will not impact only the speaker, but the hearer as well.

An old Chinese proverb says, "A rumor goes in one ear and out many mouths." The damage inflicted on the Body of Christ by wagging tongues cannot even begin to be calculated. Even a cursory look at the biblical Proverbs shows how wrong it is to pass along those accusations.

He who covers over an offense promotes love, but

whoever repeats the matter separates close friends (Proverbs 17:9).

A man who lacks judgment derides his neighbor, but a man of understanding holds his tongue (Proverbs 11:12).

Personally, I don't want to be known as one who lacks judgment or separates close friends. Perhaps it is a better choice to hold the tongue.

Often when I have taught about unity in the Church, after the meeting someone will approach me and ask to talk. Invariably these conversations lead to a horrendous story of things that happened at their former church. What the person is generally looking for is my approval for them to be an exception to the principles I have just taught. Their attitude could be summed up like this: "My situation is so far removed from anything anyone else has ever gone through that I clearly could not have been wrong when I violated the principles you've just shared." They honestly think that since they have been the recipient of unrighteous treatment, they should be entitled to strike back.

The reality is that if I shared all the true scenarios I have encountered of shameful treatment toward one another in churches, no publisher would publish the book. It would be too hot to handle. I remember years ago sitting in a hotel room with a ministry colleague discussing the situation we had just encountered in the church where we were ministering as guests. He looked at me and asked, "Do you think we should write a book about the things we've seen?"

"No," I responded, "no one would ever believe it."[6]

Perhaps you've been hurt or wronged by someone else in the Church. Maybe you've survived some less-than-positive treatment from the Body of Christ. If this describes you then you absolutely must understand that these things do not give you the right to lash out or retaliate. Someone else acting unscripturally does not give you the right to act unscripturally.

Our retaliatory attitudes are in stark contrast to the words of Jesus. He clearly told us that if someone slaps us on one cheek, we should let him slap the other one also (Matthew 5:39). Jesus went on to say, "Love your enemies and pray for those who persecute you" (Matthew 5:44).

I actually began teaching on the topic of unity and relationships several years ago after encountering a woman who was horrendously divisive. Undoubtedly, she was one of the most notorious terrorists I have ever encountered. When she was confronted by the church leadership about her behavior, even listing specific people she had talked with and situations she had created did not dissuade her. Showing her scripture after scripture that clearly said her actions were wrong in God's sight did not stop her. She left the church and continued her accusations to nearly anyone who would listen.

To this day I am amazed that an otherwise seemingly mature Christian woman could be so terribly blinded to the truth. She had been raised in a Christian home and had walked with the Lord for many years. However, she had seen the specks in the eyes of others—of course, ignoring the log in her own—and went after them with all the terrorist fire-power she could find. The devastation left behind was awful. Like in the opening story of this book, I honestly believe that Julie's mental picture of the bodies strewn about the fellow-ship hall was not too far-fetched. This is the devastation we can create when we act like terrorists.

A far better scenario is to talk through differences. Perhaps we may still arrive at a point where we realize that, this side of heaven, we may not see eye-to-eye on a particular topic. That's okay. Rather than blasting one another because we disagree, Jesus said we should love one another. Let's walk through those situations lovingly and gently, committed to one another and to our congregation.

EpiloGue

Let me offer a couple of closing thoughts. First, perhaps you've seen yourself in a new light as you've read this book. Maybe in some measure you have been guilty of being a terrorist in your own church. It could have been a recent event or maybe something from the past. In any case, you've seen the error. That's great. Recognizing the sin is the first major step. You still need to repent and ask God to forgive you. In addition you may also need to go to a person (or people) involved and ask them for forgiveness.

Second, hopefully by now you recognize that the principles of positive interaction with one another are not just good ideas. They are mandated by God's Word. Jesus said, "Love one another." Paul calls us "the Body of Christ." Peter said, "Above all, love each other deeply." Are these just nice words to fill some space in the pages of Scripture or are these concepts that should permeate how we live? I hope that by now you know the answer is obvious.

In his book *God's Dream Team*, Tommy Tenney made this observation:

> Someone said, "If the world knew we would love unconditionally and stand by one another no matter what, we would have to build thousands of new churches to accommodate all the new people..." India's great Hindu leader, Ghandi, once said, "I would have become a Christian were it not for observing Christians."[1]

How did Jesus phrase it? "By this shall all men know that you are my disciples, if you *love one another*" (John 13:35). Our witness to the world has too often been compromised because we have not demonstrated that love. We have acted like terrorists, undermining and destroying the Body of Christ.

Some time ago I read an article that shared from a historical perspective about how cultures decline. The author had identified three descending steps that a society takes in losing its foundation and strength. The first step is when people formulate their most noble ideals and make some attempt to live by them. The second step is that those people begin to realize their ideals—the standards they have set—are pretty high. This means that either they will need to change how they live or change what they believe. The third and final step occurs when the people make the decision that changing their lives is too difficult, so instead, they will change their ideals, their beliefs. The really disturbing part of this entire scenario is that after these three steps occur, the entire process starts over only on a lower plane.

As Christians, we do not seem to be disturbed by the lack of unity in the Church. In condoning this shortage of love and unity we have relegated our existence to a lower plane. We say that unity is a priority. However, our lives betray our true beliefs on this subject. We are too often unwilling to *live* the priority, so instead we lower our standard and accept something that is far below the scriptural ideal.

We too frequently do not recognize that there is anything wrong with our thinking or our actions. So what if we don't love some of our brothers and sisters in Christ? What's the big deal?

If our thinking or actions don't line up with Scripture, they are wrong. We need our minds renewed. Paul told us, "Be transformed by the renewing of your mind" (Romans 12:2b). We need to ask God to cause our minds to be renewed to be in line with His Word. We must do more than simply ask, though. We must take deliberate steps to help bring about that transformation.

Undoubtedly, the most important step would be reading and meditating on God's Word, especially the sections that deal with believers loving each other and being in unity with one another. These lofty ideals must become part of our thinking, changing our minds enough to cause us to live the ideals.

The book of Acts offers a wonderful goal for which we can aim. "All the believers were one in heart and mind" (Acts 4:32a). Oh that all the members of the Body of Christ were truly one in heart and mind!

By God's grace, let's take Peter's admonition seriously, when he told us, "*Above all*, love each other deeply" (1 Peter 4:8). Let's truly act like the Body of Christ and stand with our brothers and sisters.

Notes

Chapter 4

1. T. Davis Bunn, *The Amber Room*, Minneapolis, Minnesota: Bethany House Publishers, 1992.

Chapter 5

1. Norman Willis, *Unity With a Return*, Kirkland, WA: Christ Church Publishing, 1994.

2. Robert Moeller, *Love in Action*, Sisters, OR: Multnomah Books, 1994.

Chapter 6

1. Philip Yancey, *Soul Survivor*, New York, New York: Doubleday, 2001.

Chapter 7

1. Stephen Lawhead, *Avalon*, New York, New York: Avon Books, 1999.

Chapter 8

1. Yes, I know that many people today leave churches as a result of job transfers. Let me say two things about this. First, the majority of job transfers are not mandated by the employer. They are voluntary, and are accepted because of a salary increase. Given my choice between maintaining close relationships with the people in our church and making a few more dollars per week, for me there is no choice. Secondly, the number of people changing churches because of job transfers is relatively small compared with those who leave because of being disgruntled.

2. *The Pastor's Weekly Briefing*, Vol. 6, No. 14, April 3, 1998.

3. John Bevere, *The Bait of Satan*, Lake Mary, Florida: Charisma House, 1994, 1997.

4. Joshua Harris, *Stop Dating the Church*, Sisters, Oregon: Multnomah Publishers, 2004.

5. Bill Hull, *Building High Commitment in a Low Commitment World*, Grand Rapids, Michigan: Fleming H. Revell, 1995.

6. A well-known secular fictional author recently said that the difference between writing fiction and non-fiction is that fiction has to be believable.

Epilogue

1. Tommy Tenney, *God's Dream Team*, Ventura, California: Regal Books, 1999.

Appendix

The flow charts on the following pages are designed to help members of the congregation know how to walk through a difficult situation with a leader. Handling these scenarios in a godly way is crucial. I pray this information will prove beneficial to you and your church.

What to Do When You Disagree with a Leader

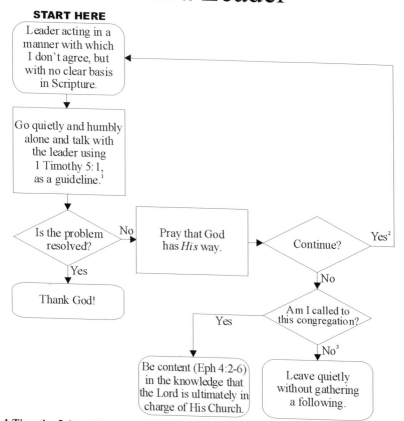

START HERE

Leader acting in a manner with which I don't agree, but with no clear basis in Scripture.

Go quietly and humbly alone and talk with the leader using 1 Timothy 5:1, as a guideline.[1]

Is the problem resolved? — No → Pray that God has *His* way. → Continue? — Yes[2]

Yes ↓

Thank God!

Continue? — No ↓

Am I called to this congregation?

Yes → Be content (Eph 4:2-6) in the knowledge that the Lord is ultimately in charge of His Church.

No[3] → Leave quietly without gathering a following.

1 Timothy 5:1 — "Do not rebuke an older man harshly, but exhort him as if he were your father."

Ephesians 4:2-6 — "Be completely humble and gentle; be patient, bearing with one another in love. Make every effort to keep the unity of the Spirit through the bond of peace. There is one body and one Spirit–just as you were called–one Lord, one faith, one baptism; one God and Father of all, who is over all and through all and in all."

1. Please note that running away from the situation at this point is not a biblical option.
2. It should go without saying, but I'll say it anyway: 1 Timothy 5:1 is still in effect the second (or third or...) time around.
3. If you honestly believe that God is sovereign (if you don't, read Acts 17:26 and other related passages) then you had better have some *very* compelling reasons for making this choice (something much more substantial than, "I'm just not comfortable here.").

What to Do When a Leader Acts in a Sinful Manner

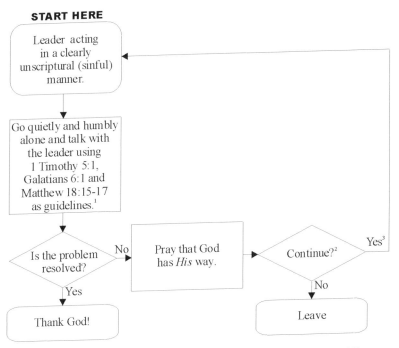

START HERE

Leader acting in a clearly unscriptural (sinful) manner.

↓

Go quietly and humbly alone and talk with the leader using 1 Timothy 5:1, Galatians 6:1 and Matthew 18:15-17 as guidelines.[1]

Is the problem resolved? — No → Pray that God has *His* way. → Continue?[2] — Yes[3]

Yes ↓

Thank God!

No ↓

Leave

---

1 Timothy 5:1 — "Do not rebuke an older man harshly, but exhort him as if he were your father."

Galatians 6:1 — "Brothers, if someone is caught in a sin, you who are spiritual should restore him gently. But watch yourself, or you also may be tempted."

Matthew 18:15-17 — "If your brother sins against you, go and show him his fault, just between the two of you. If he listens to you, you have won your brother over. But if he will not listen, take one or two others along, so that 'every matter may be established by the testimony of two or three witnesses.' If he refuses to listen to them, tell it to the church; and if he refuses to listen even to the church, treat him as you would a pagan or a tax collector."

1. Please note that running away from the situation at this point is not a biblical option.
2. Ephesians 5:11 talks about exposing the deeds of darkness. My hesitation in mentioning this as an option in this process is because it has been my experience that the majority of people in the North American Church are not mature enough to handle this step. Honestly, if you think you are mature enough, you're probably not.
3. Matthew 18 above does not negate the possibility of going and speaking with the person alone on more than one occasion. This can actually be a very helpful—and less threatening—idea before taking someone else along.

CHECK OUT THESE OTHER GREAT BOOKS BY TOM KRAEUTER

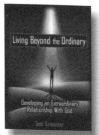

Living Beyond the Ordinary $10.00   Eternal life starts now. If we as Christians believe that Jesus came to offer us "life abundantly" then why do we of all people often feel unfulfilled, still caught up in the search for peace and contentment? Why, when we long to live a life of intimacy with our Creator, do our best attempts so often end in frustration and disillusionment? This book guides sincere Christians into a joyful relationship with the God who is waiting to transform our frustration into freedom...the freedom to live the full deep life He intended for us to have.

If Standing Together Is So Great, Why Do We Keep Falling Apart? $10.00 The church in America is missing much of the power of God because of a lack of unity. In this book Tom vows not only to give us a vision for walking in unity but specific steps to do it. According to reports from Bible-believing churches of every conceivable background from all across the nation, he has succeeded. The practical, scriptural concepts are having a major impact in the lives of believers everywhere. This concise book is both timely and profound. Don't miss it.

Oh, Grow Up! $10.00   Do you want to be more like Jesus? Unfortunately there is no switch you can flip to make that happen. So how exactly can you become more like Jesus? How can we develop a life that truly reflects the character of God? Get ready to experience the everyday miracle of becoming more like Jesus.

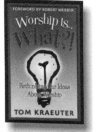

Worship Is...What?! $9.00   Tom Kraeuter invites readers to experience and enjoy the breadth and essence of biblical worship. He clearly shows that it is more important for us to see what the Bible says about this vital topic than what our traditions have dictated. In h usual story-filled way, Tom makes the Scriptures come alive for today. If you want to understand what worship is all about—or if you think you already do—you should read this book.

To order visit our web site:
www.training-resources.org

Call about quantity discounts.

Or call:
888-333-1724
M-F, 9:00-4:00 CST
(charge card orders only)

Or write to:
Training Resources
8929 Old LeMay Ferry Rd.
Hillsboro MO 63050

Postage & Packa
1 items:
2-3 items:
4-5 items:

Keys to Becoming an Effective Worship Leader $10.00 This may just be the most practical book ever written for those involved in the ministry of praise and worship. Short, concise chapters make this book easy reading while supplying powerful insights you'll refer to again and again.

Developing an Effective Worship Ministry $10.00
A hands-on practical, A-Z handbook to develop the ministry of praise and worship in the local church. You'll find a wealth of information. Whether you're a beginner or a seasoned veteran, you'll refer to it over and over.

The Worship Leader's Handbook $10.00
The question-and-answer format makes this book immensely practical. You'll find help sections on the worship leader, relationship to the congregation and to the pastor, leading worship, the worship ministry team and more.

These are some of the most practical books available for worship leaders. They will inspire you and give you a solid foundation for the ministry of praise and worship.

Things They Didn't Teach Me in Worship Leading School $12.00 Here are the experiences of 50 prominent worship leaders from around the world packed into one encouraging and insightful book. This hot-selling book features stories from Paul Baloche, Darlene Zschech, Graham Kendrick, and many others.

Times of Refreshing $15.00 A devotional book for worship ministries. 100 biblical, practical, life-related devotions to strengthen your church's worship ministry. Be refreshed as veteran worship leaders draw upon Scripture and their vast and varied experience to encourage and equip you in your calling.

Guiding Your Church Through a Worship Transition $10.00 How do you practically lead your church through a change in worship styles? Here's help! Based on solid scriptural principles and the experiences of scores of churches, this practical resource equips you with answers that will make a difference. Draw on a wealth of tested solutions and steadfast counsel, all aimed to help you build confidently, in unity, on the foundation of Christ.

All prices subject to change.

Did you find this book worthwhile? Would you like others in your church to read it also?

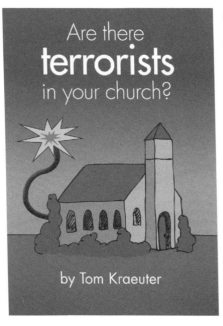